Come Listen to My Quilts

★ PLAYFUL PROJECTS ★ MIX & MATCH DESIGNS

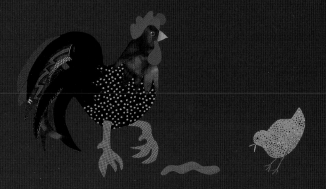

KRISTINA BECKER

WITH INGRID BECKER

C&T PUBLISHING

© 2002 Kristina Becker
Editor: Beate Marie Nellemann
Technical Editor: Carolyn Aune
Copy Editors: Lee Jonsson and Lucy Grijalva
Cover Designer: Kristen Yenche
Design Director/Book Designer: Kristen Yenche
Illustrator: Aliza Kahn Shalit
Production Assistant: Jeffery Carrillo
Published by C&T Publishing, Inc., P.O. Box 1456, Lafayette, California 94549
Front Cover: *Alley Cat* by Kristina Becker. Photography by Jim Ferreira
Back Cover: *Wormhunt* by Kristina Becker. Photography by Jim Ferreira

Attention Teachers: C&T Publishing, Inc. encourages you to use this book as a text for teaching. Contact us at 1-800-284-1114 or www.ctpub.com for more information about the C&T Teachers Program.

Library of Congress Cataloging-in-Publication Data
Becker, Kristina,
  Come listen to my quilts : playful projects, mix & match designs / Kristina Becker with Ingrid Becker.
      p. cm.
Includes index.
  ISBN 1-57120-129-7 (paper trade)
  1. Appliqué—Patterns. 2. Quilts—Design. I. Becker, Ingrid, II. Title.
  TT779 . B4 2002
  746.46'041—dc21
                          2001006583

Printed in China
10 9 8 7 6 5 4 3 2 1

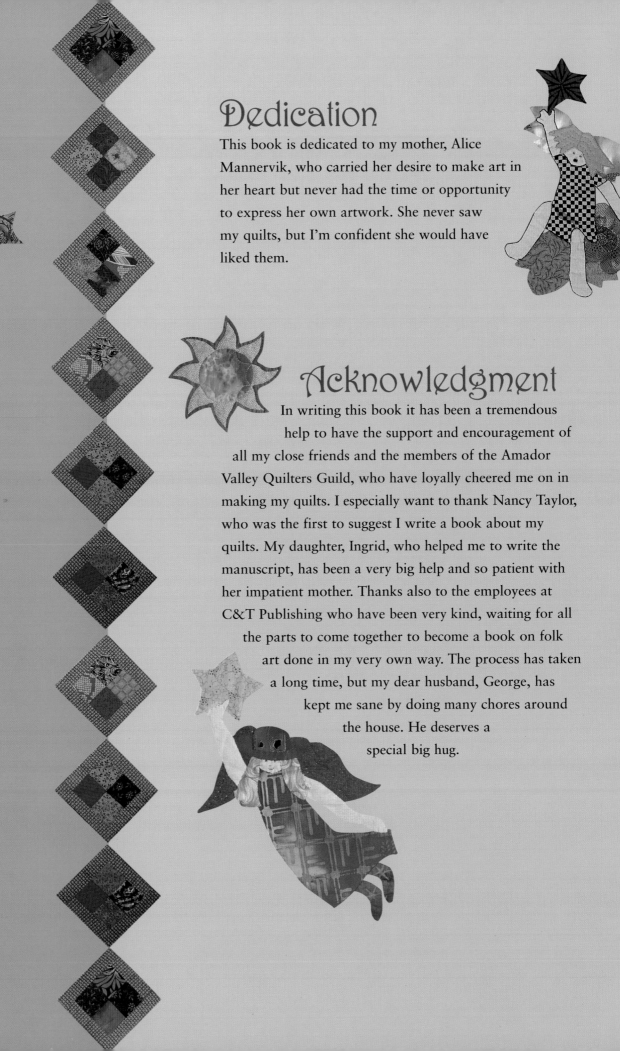

Dedication

This book is dedicated to my mother, Alice Mannervik, who carried her desire to make art in her heart but never had the time or opportunity to express her own artwork. She never saw my quilts, but I'm confident she would have liked them.

Acknowledgment

In writing this book it has been a tremendous help to have the support and encouragement of all my close friends and the members of the Amador Valley Quilters Guild, who have loyally cheered me on in making my quilts. I especially want to thank Nancy Taylor, who was the first to suggest I write a book about my quilts. My daughter, Ingrid, who helped me to write the manuscript, has been a very big help and so patient with her impatient mother. Thanks also to the employees at C&T Publishing who have been very kind, waiting for all the parts to come together to become a book on folk art done in my very own way. The process has taken a long time, but my dear husband, George, has kept me sane by doing many chores around the house. He deserves a special big hug.

Table of

Contents

Introduction

I make my quilts pretty much as I cook—right out of the shopping bags. I gather my ingredients and my selection of fabrics and then cut, cut, cut, chop, chop, chop. After the first part is done, there are long hours of simmering and thinking and rearranging until it pleases me and I can begin. The ideas for quilts come from inside me and I make up patterns as I go along. Most are spontaneous and cut freehand, then appliquéd. Often I'll design parts of the quilt while I'm working on it.

People tell me they love the stories that the birds and cats in my quilts have to tell. The simple shapes tell stories about relationships—emotions and feelings that really relate to humans. Portraying the tension between cats and birds is not as personally threatening to depict as conflicts between humans. Cats and birds are simple and direct. They're also easier to draw. I don't set out to put deep meaning into my quilts; I just love to make them. Sometimes it takes me a long time to finish a quilt. I have to wait until the whole story is "told." There must always be something happening in my quilt—something sly and funny—that adds an element of surprise and challenges the viewer to figure out for herself what's going on.

This book is a departure from the many how-to quilting manuals. My hope is that by sharing information about how I work, other quilters will be inspired to create their personal style. When I first began quilting, I studied a lot of quilts in books and at quilt shows. I decided mine would be different. I began with some traditional patterns like basket quilts, then added my own appliquéd flowers and vines. I wanted the quilts to state that I, Kristina Becker, made this particular quilt. I don't want my quilts to copy something that has been done before. Life is too short to regress to another time.

My art is an extension of my lifelong habit of doing my own thing. As a folk artist I'm my own critic. If I've made a quilt that pleases me, it makes little difference what the judges at a show say. I make quilts for my own satisfaction and joy, and some of the work is quite rebellious. I really don't mind kicking sand in the face of the viewer.

I don't have formal art training, just a lifelong passion for needlework, painting, doll making, and other crafts. As a child growing up in Sweden, I learned to love handmade things made from the heart. Back then I didn't know the term "folk art" even though I was surrounded by it.

My parents, Cyrus and Alice Mannervik, were teachers in our small town but they both had many other skills. My father was a woodworker, poet, and author who wrote children's books and plays. In the summer he painted. My mother loved to do needlework, and she embroidered beautiful monograms on towels and sheets, crocheted lace, and knitted. At Christmas my brother, Svante, and I eagerly anticipated the handmade gifts we all gave one another. We were always encouraged to make our own patterns and drawings.

Rainy days were a treat for me because it meant I had all the time I could wish for to create things. Sometimes I wanted a coloring book, but my mother always discouraged that thought by telling me she liked my hand drawings much better. Eventually, I learned to appreciate my own work and individuality.

This concept of learning to cultivate and appreciate your unique style is what I want to convey to other quilters. Be patient with yourself and learn to love your work, the colors you choose, and the individual way you design your quilts. Some people like very simple, cookie-cutter designs while others prefer the lovely Baltimore-style patterns. I say, why repeat designs from a century ago? You can make just-as-lovely quilts today using your very own patterns and colors. If I worked from a pattern or someone else's design, I would already know how the quilt would look finished and I'd be bored.

Have fun with your designs. My own drawing skills aren't great, but I have a good time creating my crazy birds and cats. I know the basic shape of a cat and how it moves, but when I make an appliqué pattern I don't attempt to create a life-like drawing of the cats I see prowling outside my window. Sometimes I'll look at photographs of animals, but I rarely study paintings because a painting suggests a color choice, and I don't want to be influenced by someone else's interpretation. When I make a drawing for a quilt, it's usually nothing more than a rough sketch, a guideline for where to place the animals or flowers. One of my favorite quilts, called *Moonbird* (page 8), started out as a doodle. That doodle grew into a sketch, and soon I had made a quilt with an enormous bird landing among a group of outrageously colored cats. Sometimes I feel the bird is frightening the cats. Other times I feel the cats are threatening the bird. I'll leave it to someone else to figure out the true connection between these creatures.

I love color and I'm not afraid to use bright or unusual colors in my quilts. To me it's like painting a picture. Birds can be polka dot with striped legs, cats can be checked, and angels can have turquoise hair if that's what I decide to put in my picture. As I sew, I enjoy contemplating how the colors will work together. When you buy fabrics for your collection, pick colors that you like, not what your best friend chooses or what the salesclerk suggests is nice. As your collection grows you'll find the colors will start to harmonize, and everyone will recognize that these colors are ones that only you could have chosen for your quilt.

I don't get carried away with perfection. Many quilters strive for absolute perfection, but as you explore a new, freer style of quiltmaking, try to relax. Don't be too hard on yourself. It may not be perfect, but it will get better with each try. The most important thing is to enjoy your work. Just have a good time and let the joy shine through.

Gallery

While I was making this quilt, I became so engrossed in the work that I discovered something funny about it only after I had appliquéd the last sun in the corner and hung the quilt on the wall of my studio. When I noticed that I had appliquéd the moon, sun, and stars on the same quilt, I called my daughter, Ingrid, and told her I'd made a big mistake. "The sun and stars can't be visible at the same time," I moaned. "Don't worry," she said, "there aren't any cats that fly or are purple-checked either." I'm convinced that somehow this daughter of mine is older—and wiser—than I am. She always has been.

Moonbird, 1993, 51" x 52".
Photo by Jim Ferreira.

Birdwatching, detail.
Photo by Jim Ferreira.

Cats like to hide—they hope the birds won't see them. I wanted to make these birds colorful and loud. The tree is barely big enough to hold all the birds. The large, menacing cat below is waiting for them.

Birdwatching, 1997, 50" x 60".
Photo by Jim Ferreira.

Cats are one of my favorite quilt subjects. They are so aloof and sly. This black and white "tuxedo" cat keeps a close watch on the birds around him. Sometimes I'll make a pieced border with lots of colors just to play with fabrics and exercise my piecing skills. I don't worry about matching colors perfectly. Sometimes a quilt just has to set your teeth on edge. Otherwise, it's too boring and predictable.

Tuxedo Cat, 1993, 44" x 41".
Photo by Jim Ferreira.

The older I get, the freer I become in my design and use of color. On this quilt, I decided not to use foundation piecing for the squares, but instead set the strips together as they were cut out. The work was fun and the strong colors seemed to sing under my hands. I kept going until I had enough squares for a small quilt and then I noticed some of the squares weren't perfectly even. I had a little pang of guilt, but not for long. Even though I grew up believing the work had to be perfect, I've learned to break loose. As usual, the birds in this quilt have to make decisions. Are they going to eat the fuzzy worm or the fallen apple first?

The Tree, 1999, 44" x 44".
Photo by Jim Ferreira.

This cat had already used up one of his nine lives before he landed on this wallhanging. I'd used this design on a fairly large pillow in the late 1970s. He looks a little surprised, and maybe even a bit guilty, for having caught the mouse.

Cat and Mouse, 1995, 13" x 17".
Photo by Jim Ferreira.

While I was making the larger quilt on page 14, I pinned on so many leaves that I got really confused. I wanted to see how many varied leaves the design could hold so I made this test square to play with the pattern and composition. The branches for the leaves are $1/4$" sashings between the blocks. Some of the leaves are pieced, while others are appliquéd onto another fabric so it forms an edge around the leaf. It's more work for greater effect.

Bird, 1991, 33" x 33".
Photo by Sharon Risedorph.

Eight Birds and One Cat, 1991, 53" x 53".
Photo by Tristan Hoagland.

One day I drew these funky birds just for fun. I appliquéd them on a dark, striped fabric with the stripes going in different directions. I like to make cats from different prints, especially checks. This cat looked so pleased with himself that my son, Eric, suggested I add a loose feather in the square with the missing bird.

Sometimes I'll design a quilt with a particular fabric in mind. I had some wonderful wool fabric in fine dress weight that I wanted to use for a quilt, so I made a rough sketch of a quilt with red stars and a folkart vine as a decoration. But a piece of strong blue fabric kept calling to me as if to say, "Choose me instead; I'm more fun and colorful." I listened to that little voice and allowed myself to be persuaded. I took the design and turned the red wool stars into vibrant yellow stars on black backgrounds. That was fun to do. Next, my elegant, muted folkloric vines in gray and olive green became cherry trees.

This quilt took on a life and personality all its own and I just followed along for the ride. The tree roots weren't particularly interesting, but fortunately a cat came along to walk in front of one of the trees. The cat had to have a purpose and so there is a bird pulling on a big, green worm. Then it seemed the stars were pretty static, so in order to add some "twinkle" I let some smaller stars fall into the tree. One of them just happened to have a little angel hanging on to it. The fact that she had turquoise hair was no problem. The quilt needed a turquoise touch in there anyway. Besides, if you're an angel you can have any hair color you want.

I call this quilt *September* because the strong blue color reminds me of the intense blue skies we saw in Sweden during that month. In September the trees still have the last of the fruit on the branches. It's one of my favorite months and this is one of my favorite quilts.

September, detail.
Photo by Tristan Hoagland.

September, 1993, 65" x 52". Owned by Kay Melchor and David Bieselin.
Photo by Tristan Hoagland.

"Fallen" Angel, 1995, 33" x 46".
Photo by Jim Ferreira.

It was so much fun working with the little angel with the turquoise hair and so many people enjoyed seeing her on *September* (page 15) that I had to include her on another quilt. I dreamed up this quilt in the middle of my annual gardening spurt, and this sunflower is how I envisioned the ones in my garden would grow. The little angel has landed on a flower and the hens are coming to investigate. "How come she's here?" the hens are asking themselves. "I thought she stayed with the cat."

Across the street from my kitchen window is a large field where many crows gather. Most crows are social birds, but one day I noticed a crow who preferred to be off by himself, walking in the gutter and looking for treasures. The crow was so close to us that my husband, George, and I noticed what extraordinarily large feet this particular bird had. I drew this crow with the exaggerated feet and then appliquéd him onto a quilt. Scraps of a favorite blue fabric together with leftover flowers from my *Barnyard* quilt (page 54) and some simple vines made the border.

The Neighborhood Crow, 1995, 44" x 40".
Photo by Jim Ferreira.

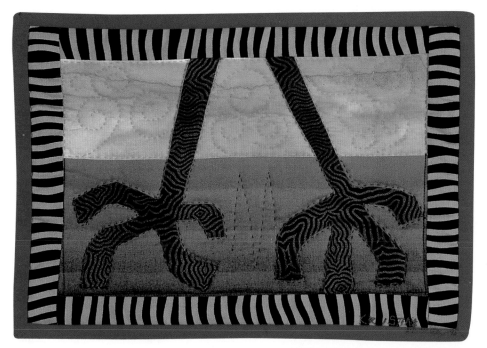

At This Price You Only Get the Feet, 1995, 10" x 7".
Photo by Jim Ferreira.

As a joke I made two smaller versions of the crow quilt. First I took the full-size crow and put him in a very crowded space. The bird's whole body doesn't even fit in the space. I was laughing to myself as I finished the quilt. I don't know if other quilters laugh about their quilts, but I like to put some humor in mine. While I was still laughing about *Crowded Crow* I made an even smaller quilt with just the feet of the big crow. I love to design outrageous feet on the birds in my quilts. Many people have told me they especially love the feet on my birds, so here they are.

Crowded Crow, 1995, 10" x 13".
Photo by Jim Ferreira.

This quilt was inspired by the colors in the Pennsylvania Dutch quilts and other folk art. I wanted to use the strong yellows, greens, and reds that I had seen in books about these quilts. I wanted the strong yellow to be the "neutral" background and from there it was easy to pour on the other colors and enjoy. The circles were cut free-hand and appliquéd. I want my work to show that my hand has worked the quilt, not a machine that would make it perfect.

Four Black Birds, 1992, 61" x 61".
Photo by Sharon Risedorph.

Starcatch, detail.
Photo by Jim Ferreira.

On a trip to Nova Scotia, my husband, George, and I saw some wonderful houses. Some were painted purple with fuchsia trim and others were dark gold with turquoise trim. I just loved the colorful houses and decided to include them in a quilt inspired by old Swedish wallhangings. These painted wallhangings depict Biblical parables, with the characters all dressed in traditional Swedish folk costumes or in fashions of the times. My version has angels dressed in contemporary clothes. Instead of Biblical houses, these houses are from Nova Scotia.

Starcatch, 1993, 40" x 43".
Photo by Jim Ferreira.

This quilt deals with relationships and is one of the few serious quilts I've made. The idea for this quilt came to me after my husband, George, described how he'd watched a cat being "chased" away by birds on the back-yard fence. I intended to tell only the story of a small bird chasing a cat, yet as the work progressed, I saw the parallels to my own life and this quilt came to symbolize an emotionally difficult time for our family. It was healing to work on this quilt, but I've never displayed it in our home. Maybe someday I will.

Moving On, 1994, 55" x 66".
Photo by Jim Ferreira.

After having sewn for many years on various projects, I found myself with quite a few leftover Nine-Patches and strips from Log Cabin blocks. One day I just pieced them all together to make six 12" x 12" blocks. Because the fabrics were all in my favorite colors, the blocks harmonized well. I chose one of my bird patterns to fit in the bluish purple sky and the little angel came along for the ride. They landed on the moon, our latest "colony." The machine quilting, by Kim Jagger, was done in a fireworks motif using Sulky thread.

Visiting Our Newest "Colony," detail.
Photo by Jim Ferreira.

Visiting Our Newest "Colony", 2001, 38" x 46".
Photo by Jim Ferreira.

In "courtship" the male bird is so full of love and passion that his beak is swollen. Like many females, the female bird here is acting coy and playing hard to get. In "family" there is always the one child who must do things his or her own way and who marches to the tune of a different drummer. By the time we arrive at "retirement," many times life has taken different turns for us, and we are not always even looking in the same direction all the time.

Stages of Life: Courtship, Family, and Retirement, 1995, 34" x 51".
Photo by Jim Ferreira.

Getting Started Exercise

This exercise is for you to make a simple folk art design. I have intentionally not included a photograph for reference in order not to stifle your creativity. I've included some basic guidelines to help you along in making decisions. For general instructions on appliqué techniques and embroidery stitches, please refer to the Toolbox beginning on page 30.

I try to use color for maximum effect. If, for example, I'm making a flower or a vine, I'll choose many shades of red for the petals and many colors besides green for the leaves. This way the appliqué "glitters" like sunlight on plants. Once you start studying flowers and bushes you'll see how many different colors and shapes there are. Nature is endlessly varied. Leaves on a bush appear almost rust brown when they first come out in spring. Later they turn varying shades of green.

I don't use shadowing in my appliqué, only different colors to help make them sparkle. Stems can be striped in wild colors, and birds and animals are made from whatever color or pattern I feel is needed for that particular part of the quilt or composition. This mixing and matching makes for a livelier, more colorful picture.

You may want to enlarge the patterns by hand or on a photocopy machine. Choose the size you most prefer to work with. Remember that with folk art the proportions for your designs are totally up to you. The same goes for color. Work with colors that you like. Think about what season you want to show in the picture. If you're including animals in the scene, think about their placement: Do they appear to communicate with each other? Is there some interaction between them? Are they friendly or aggressive? How are they relating to the other subjects in the motif? Are they among the flowers or in the grass? Are they far away or close up?

Start with five to ten pieces of fabric. Ask yourself questions about what you would like to do next. Do you want to have a lake or grass, or maybe a meadow? Is it night or day? What is the season? Pick fabrics accordingly.

CREATING YOUR OWN QUILT

1 fat quarter for the sky

1 fat quarter for the ground

1 fat quarter for the tree

1 fat quarter for the cat,

Assorted scraps for leaves, birds, and flowers

Refer to page 30 for appliqué instructions.

1. Sew the sky and ground pieces together first to make a horizon.

2. Enlarge the tree pattern on page 29 to the size you would like and copy it onto a piece of fabric. Then cut it out and place it on the background fabric. Place the tree with the roots below the horizon line.

3. Once the "naked" tree is in place you can dress it with leaves. I've designed some basic leaves for you to use. Enlarge them to the size you need. Cut the shapes the size you like, trying to capture the basic shapes of leaves. Then simplify them in order to work them into an appliqué. I sometimes use an index card to make my leaf templates.

the leaves on using fusible web, or glue them on with a fabric glue stick. For a denser tree, add more leaves. Just don't forget to leave some space for birds, fruits, or blossoms.

4. Pick out and enlarge a bird shape that you like or draw your own. If the birds are big, you may need only a few. Place the birds on the branches of the tree. If you make them all the same color, you'll have a flock of birds. When you place the birds, remember they have wings! If they are spread open, the birds are flying into the tree.

LEAF

GINKGO LEAF

Start with ten to fifteen leaves. Use varied colors, including both lights and darks, to make the tree come alive. If you've never worked in such a free method, you can start by arranging the leaves on the tree using tiny pins. Then iron

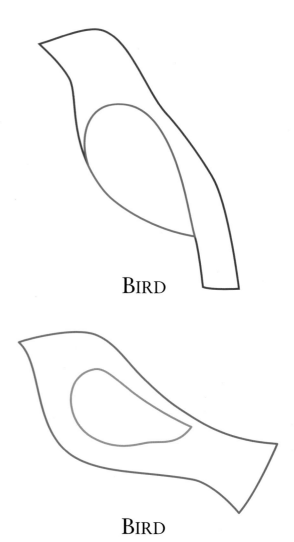

BIRD

BIRD

5. Flowers add another spark to the tree. I've included some flower shapes for you to start with. Enlarge the patterns if needed. Choose a color that will stand out among the leaves. Use simple shapes like circles or triangles for the petals. I've used buttons for flowers in some of my trees.

BRANCH WITH FRENCH KNOT FLOWERS

FLOWER

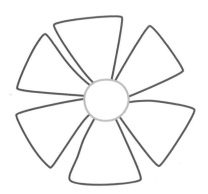

FLOWER

One day before I made the quilt *Moving On* (page 21), I came across a dress shop that was going out of business. I picked up some silk-covered buttons that became the fruit or blossoms on the tree branch hanging over the cat. Cherries are very common in folk art, probably because they are so easy to make and so decorative.

BRANCH WITH CHERRIES

You can use a dime to make a template for the cherries. Cut out the cherry with a seam allowance, then baste around the edge of the circle, gather the circle, and pull the thread tight over the template. Press. Remove the template, then take out the gathering thread. Have fun placing the cherries.

Baste.   *Gather.*

6. I also made a cat pattern (page 29) that you can include in your scene. Enlarge him to the size you want. Make him any color you like. He can be big or small, green or purple. You can surround him with pretty, long-stemmed flowers. That way he looks as though he's walking in a garden.

You will find more inspirational patterns in the Toolbox beginning on page 30.

FLOWERS

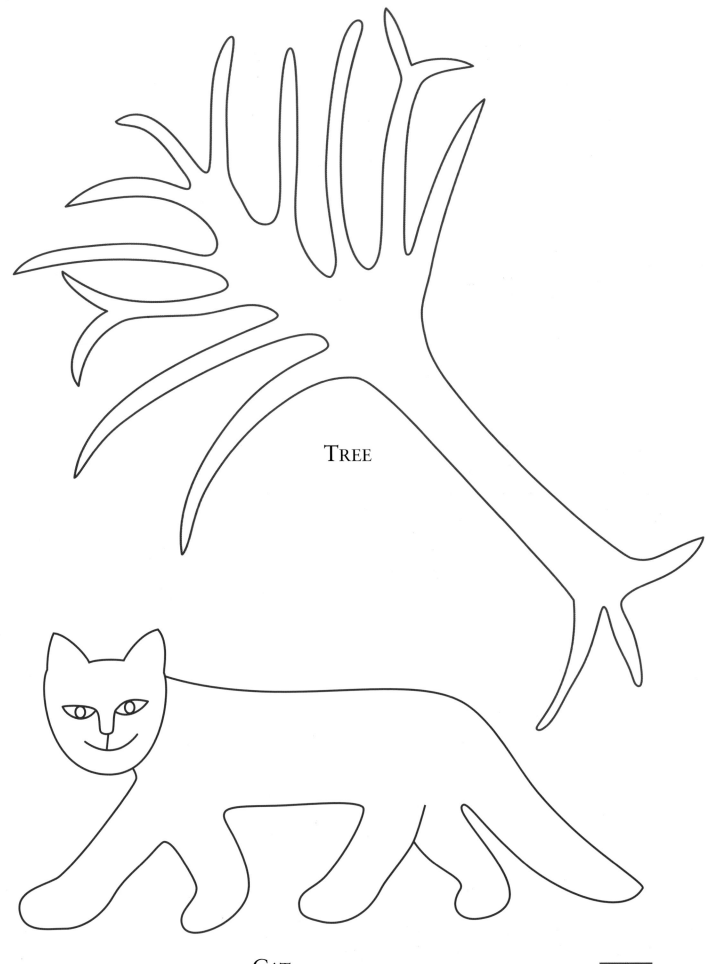

TREE

CAT

29

Toolbox

While each quilt you make is an expression of your own personality and creativity, quilters use basic tools to convert their designs into quilts. In this chapter I've included some of the tools that I use when I make my quilts. Use the techniques and patterns in this chapter as a guide while you are designing and making your own quilts.

APPLIQUÉ

Machine Appliqué Using Fusible Adhesive

Trace the patterns onto the paper side of the fusible web. Be sure to reverse the patterns if necessary. Following the manufacturer's instructions, fuse the traced patterns to the wrong side of the appliqué fabric. It helps to use an appliqué pressing sheet to avoid getting the adhesive on your iron or ironing board. Cut out the pieces along the pencil line.

Remove the paper and position the appliqué piece on your project. Be sure the web (rough) side is down. Fuse in place, following the manufacturer's instructions. Stitch if desired.

Needle-Turn Appliqué

This is a great technique when using simple shapes. Very little preparation is needed and it is easy to achieve the desired shape by folding on the drawn line.

Create your shape out of cardboard or template plastic. Place the template on the right side of your fabric and trace around the shape with a pencil or water-soluble marker. Trim the fabric $3/16"$-$1/4"$ around the outside drawn line and you are ready to appliqué.

To needle-turn appliqué, fold under a small section of the edge. Bring the needle up from the back of the fabric, and catch one or two threads on the underside of the fold. Insert the needle directly down through the background fabric and pull through to the wrong side, so that the stitch is concealed.

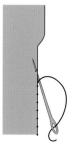

You will find patterns for appliqué designs on pages 26-29, 33, and 36. They will give you ideas to begin your own designs.

PAPER PIECING

Once you get used to it, paper piecing is an easy way to ensure that your blocks will be accurate. You sew on the side of the paper with the printed lines. Fabric is placed with the right side up on the non-printed side.

1. Trace or photocopy the number of paper-piecing patterns needed for your project.

2. Use a smaller-than-usual stitch length (1.5–1.8 or 18–20 stitches per inch), and a slightly larger needle (size 90/14). This makes the paper removal easier and will result in tighter stitches that can't be pulled apart when you tear the paper off.

3. Cut the pieces slightly larger than necessary—about $1/4$"–$1/2$" larger or more for triangles; they do not need to be perfect shapes.

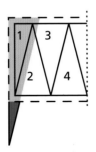 *With paper piecing you don't have to worry about the grain of the fabric. You are sewing on paper and that stabilizes the block. The paper is not torn off until after the blocks are sewn together.*

4. Follow the number sequence when piecing. Pin piece #1 in place on the blank side of the paper. Hold the paper up to the light to make sure the piece covers the area, with the seam allowance amply covered.

5. Fold the pattern back at the stitching line and trim the fabric to a $1/4$" seam allowance.

6. Cut piece #2 large enough to cover the area of #2 plus a generous seam allowance. It's a good idea to cut each piece larger than you think necessary; it might be a bit wasteful, but it is easier than ripping out tiny stitches! Align the edge with the trimmed seam allowance of piece #1, right sides together, and pin. Turn paper side up and sew on the line.

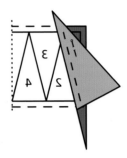

7. Open piece #2 and press.

8. Continue sewing each piece in order, being sure to fold back the paper pattern and trim the seam allowance to $1/4$" before adding the next piece.

9. Trim all around the finished unit to the $1/4$" seam allowance. Leave the paper intact until all the blocks have been sewn together, then carefully remove it. Creasing the paper at the seam line helps when tearing it.

EMBROIDERY

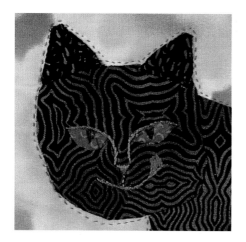

Blanket Stitch

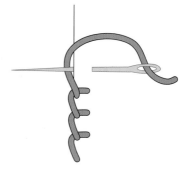

Blanket stitch

French Knot

French knot

Satin Stitch

Satin stitch

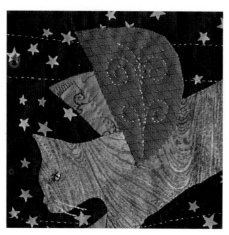

Stem Stitch

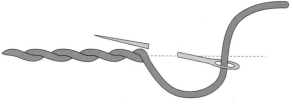

Stem stitch

BORDERS

Borders can really show off the center of the quilt. I have fun making my borders and some-times I even start by designing the border first. You will find some border patterns here that you can use as tools to get you started in creating your own border designs.

SUN PATTERN FOR BORDER

Enlarge as desired.

STAR PATTERN FOR BORDER

Enlarge as desired.

PAPER-PIECED BORDER

Enlarge as desired.

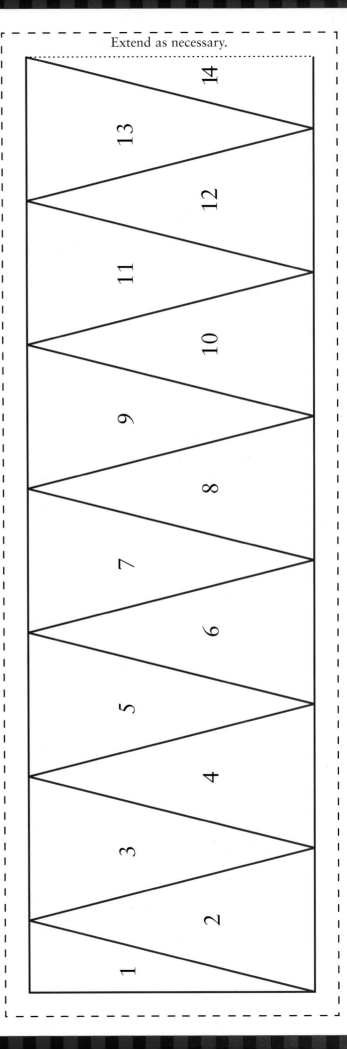

Extend as necessary.

QUILTING

Quilting Designs

Quilting designs are a wonderful place to let your personal style shine. I happen to be averse to stippling. I feel stippling turns a quilt into a mattress pad. Instead, I like swirls and soft lines that I draw freehand on the fabric with a water-soluble ink pen. This way I see where the quilting should be placed. When I'm drawing the design I feel like I'm doing calligraphy.

Quilting Stitches

I choose to hand quilt. I prefer quilting with contrasting color thread, often red. When I first started quilting I was very proper and chose only matching thread. One day my husband commented that it was a real shame nobody could see the nice even stitches. After that I started experimenting with red quilting thread and found that I liked the effect so much better. Later I tried perle cotton thread and the effect was even more dramatic.

I use stab-stitching with a medium darning needle when I'm working with the heavier thread. Taking one stitch at a time goes almost as fast as rocking with a regular needle. I put the needle straight down into the quilt. Then I pull it all the way through and push it straight back up to make a stitch.

Marking Your Quilt

My favorite method of marking a quilt top is to use bridal tulle. First I draw the design on paper with a permanent marker. Next I cover the design with waxed paper or plastic so that I can use it again. After that I place the tulle over the design and hold it in place with masking tape. I trace the design onto the tulle with a permanent marker. After the whole design is traced I can mark it onto the quilt top, with either a silver pen or a dressmaker's pencil, right through the tulle. The design shows up on either light or dark fabric.

I give you two of the patterns I use for quilting designs (page 35). Use them to help you get started, but then go ahead and create your own quilting designs to enhance your particular quilt.

FLOWER BORDER
QUILTING PATTERN

Enlarge as desired.

ANGEL QUILTING PATTERN

Enlarge as desired.

BIRD FEET

Enlarge as desired.

BIRDS

Enlarge as desired.

Alley Cat, 1998, 25½" x 25½".
Photo by Jim Ferreira.

Alley Cat

Alley Cat, detail.
Photo by Jim Ferreira.

You'd think by now it would be easy for me to make a cat quilt, but this one gave me more trouble than any of the others I'd made. The cat grew and took up more space than I'd counted on, so he swallowed the bird that was supposed to sit on a perch. The flowers grew so strong and healthy they overpowered the cat. But most difficult were the Basket blocks. I set them together wrong, I turned the points the wrong way. You name it. I did it!

Original sketch of *Alley Cat*

Just as I was about to finally give up on this quilt, my friends rescued the poor cat and brought him back to life. They helped me understand that, after all, he's just a gruesome alley cat. My quilts aren't perfect. Why should they be—I'm not!

- Fat quarter or $^3/_8$ yard for sky
- $^1/_4$ yard for grass
- $^1/_4$ yard for cat appliqué
- Assorted scraps for flowers, bird, and cat's eyes
- $^1/_8$ yard each of two fabrics for inner border
- $^1/_2$ yard total of dark scraps for Basket blocks
- $^5/_8$ yard total of light scraps for Basket blocks
- $^1/_4$ yard for binding
- 1 yard for backing
- 30" x 30" thin batting
- Embroidery thread for embellishment
- Fusible web

MAKING THE CENTER

1. For the sky, cut a piece of fabric $9\frac{1}{2}$" x $13\frac{1}{2}$". For the grass, cut a piece $4\frac{1}{2}$" x $13\frac{1}{2}$". Sew the sky and grass pieces together horizontally.

Note: Since the cat's tail overlaps the borders you may choose to either add the borders to the quilt center before stitching the appliqué or stitch the appliqué (except for the end of the cat's tail) onto the sky/grass section, then add the borders.

2. For the inner border, cut two strips $1\frac{1}{2}$" x $13\frac{1}{2}$" for top and bottom borders and two strips $1\frac{1}{2}$" x $15\frac{1}{2}$" for side borders. Add to the quilt center.

3. For the outer border, make sixteen 5" Basket blocks following the instructions, page 40.

4. Sew two strips of three baskets each for the side borders. Add to the quilt center.

5. Sew two strips of five baskets for the top and bottom borders. Add to the quilt center.

MAKING THE APPLIQUÉ

Refer to page 30 for appliqué instructions.

1. Cut out the cat, the bird in his tummy, the flowers, the stems, and the leaves using the pattern on page 41.

2. Position the cat, bird, flowers, stems, and leaves on the center piece and appliqué. For the cat's eyes, use fusible web on some green fabric. Cut out an eye shape and iron on. Draw the pupil using a permanent marker.

3. The tongue and the rest of his facial features are embroidered. See Toolbox, page 32, for instructions to make the embroidery stitches.

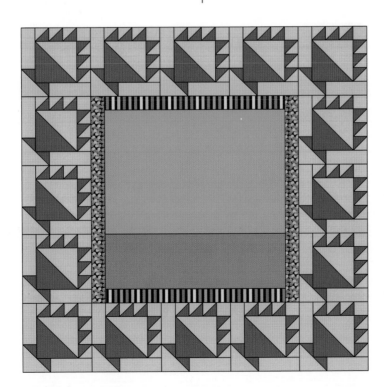

MAKING THE 5" BASKET BLOCK

Make sixteen 5" Basket blocks.

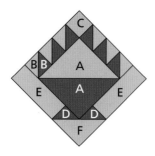

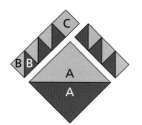

For each block cut:

A One light 3⅞" square, cut in half diagonally.

One dark 3⅞" square, cut in half diagonally.

B Four light 1⅞" squares, cut in half diagonally.

Four dark 1⅞" squares, cut in half diagonally.

C One light 1½" square.

D One dark 1⅞" square, cut in half diagonally.

E Two light 1½" x 3½" rectangles.

F One light 2⅞" square, cut in half diagonally.

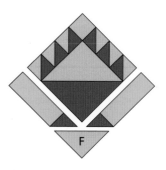

FINISHING

Layer, baste, and then either hand quilt or machine quilt the top with whatever design you like. Add binding.

FLOWER OR
PETAL
Enlarge 200%

BIRD
Enlarge 200%

LEAF
Enlarge 200%

FLOWER
Enlarge 200%

ALLEY CAT
Enlarge 200%

Wormhunt, 1996, 44$\frac{1}{2}$" x 50$\frac{1}{2}$". Owned by Margaret Termini.
Photo by Jim Ferreira.

In this quilt the birds are hunting the worms. The red bird in the top right corner is running so fast in excitement that the worm is just flapping in the wind.

I used stars like this on the border of another quilt and liked the way they looked, so I made more for this quilt. I also wanted to use some of the many blue fabrics I'd collected. Most of them were just small scraps, so they all had to get along as pieced background for my happy birds.

To make your own pieced borders on an appliqué quilt, first measure all sides of the center. Select a pieced pattern of your choice to fit the border measurements as closely as possible.

With the 4" star pattern I picked for *Wormhunt*, I found I could fit eleven stars for the top and bottom borders and twelve on each side. Even so, I was a bit short on the top and bottom borders, so I simply added a narrow border of red fabric on each side to make it even. You'll find that flexibility is key with freestyle quilts. To me, that's what is fun and challenging about working without a pattern, and it makes me a happier person.

- 2 yards of scraps for quilt center

- ¼ yard for narrow inner border

- ³⁄₈ yard for second border

- ⅛ yard for side borders

- 1 yard total of assorted scraps for border stars

- 1 yard for border star backgrounds

- ½ yard for binding

- 2³⁄₄ yards for backing

- 53" x 49" batting

- Buttons for bird eyes

43

MAKING THE CENTER

1. For the center of the quilt you can piece a background in blue fabrics as I did here. I used pieces cut anywhere from $1\frac{1}{2}$" wide to $6\frac{1}{2}$" wide, and of varying lengths. Then I sewed them together, arranging the values and prints in a way that pleased me. Trim to $29\frac{1}{2}$" x $35\frac{1}{2}$".

2. For the narrow inner border, cut two 1" x $35\frac{1}{2}$" strips for side borders and two 1" x $30\frac{1}{2}$" strips for top and bottom border. Add to the quilt center.

3. For the second border, cut two $2\frac{1}{2}$" x $36\frac{1}{2}$" strips for side borders and two $2\frac{1}{2}$" x $34\frac{1}{2}$" strips for top and bottom border. Add to the quilt center.

MAKING THE APPLIQUÉ

Refer to page 30 for appliqué instructions.

Now it's time to appliqué the birds. Cut out the birds and worms using the patterns on page 46. Their placement is up to you. I don't measure their exact distance away from each other. Some of the birds are overlapping the blue border and some are running in different directions. Add their wings and some worms. Position the pieces, then appliqué. I sewed on small buttons for their eyes.

MAKING THE 4" STAR BLOCK

For a star border like mine, you'll need forty-two 4" Star blocks.

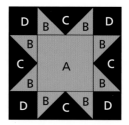

Star

For each star cut:

    A   One $2\frac{1}{2}$" square.

    B   Eight $1\frac{1}{2}$" squares.

Background:

    C   Four $1\frac{1}{2}$" x $2\frac{1}{2}$" rectangles.

    D   Four $1\frac{1}{2}$" x $1\frac{1}{2}$" squares.

1. To make star points sew B squares to the C rectangles as shown below.

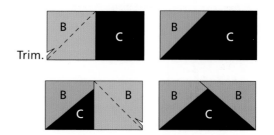

2. Sew pieces together as shown to make the star.

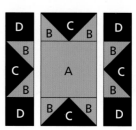

MAKING THE STAR BLOCK BORDER

1. First add the narrow side border to the quilt's center. Cut two $1^1/_2$" x $40^1/_2$" strips in a contrasting fabric of your choice and add them to the sides of the quilt center. I used bright red against the blue background.

2. Sew two strips of ten stars each for the side borders. Add to the quilt center.

3. Sew two strips of eleven stars each for the top and bottom borders. Add to the quilt center.

FINISHING

Layer, baste, and then either hand quilt or machine quilt the top with whatever design you like. Add binding.

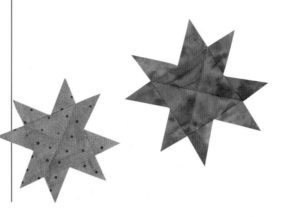

BIRD

WORM

Blackbird Pillow, 1999, 10" x 19".
Photo by Jim Ferreira.

Blackbird Pillow

- $3/8$ yard for pillow

- $1/8$ yard black or scraps for blackbirds

- Scraps for birds' wings

- Machine-embroidery thread

- Tear-away stabilizer

- Polyester stuffing

MAKING THE PILLOW

1. Cut two pieces of fabric 11" x 20" for the front and back.

2. Cut three birds—two the same and one different.

3. Cut three wings.

MAKING THE APPLIQUÉ

Refer to page 30 for appliqué instructions.

1. Appliqué the birds 1-1$1/2$" apart on the front of the pillow.

2. Add the birds' wings.

3. Machine embroider the birds' legs using a satin stitch.

FINISHING

1. With right sides together, sew the pillow front and back together, leaving an 8" opening on one side. Use a $1/2$" seam allowance.

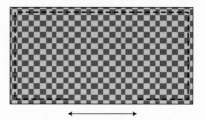

8" opening

2. Turn the pillow, stuff, and blindstitch the opening closed.

BIRD

BIRD

Sheep With Bird, 1997, 22" x 21".
Photo by Jim Ferreira.

Sheep with Bird

Sometimes I'll make a smaller quilt. There's no particular reason; I just like a different format.

On many of our driving vacations we've seen sheep in the pastures standing perfectly still with a bird resting on their backs. It's always struck me as comical, so I made this quilt that has a sheep with a black bird resting on his back. The flower was supposed to be a birdhouse, but it didn't fit in the quilt so it became a big flower instead. Things happen.

- ³/₈ yard for sky

- ¹/₄ yard for grass

- Assorted scraps for sheep, bird, and flower appliqués

- ¹/₈ yard or scrap for narrow inner border

- ¹/₈ yard for second border

- ¹/₄ yard for outer border

- ¹/₄ yard for binding

- ²/₃ yard for backing

- 24" x 25" thin batting

- Perle cotton #8 thread

- Embroidery thread

MAKING THE CENTER

1. Cut the sky fabric 12¹/₂" x 13¹/₂". Cut the grass fabric 5" x 13¹/₂". Cut points along one edge of the grass fabric to resemble grass and appliqué to the sky fabric to make a 12¹/₂" x 13¹/₂" quilt center.

2. For the narrow inner border, cut two ³/₄" x 12¹/₂" strips for the side borders and cut two ³/₄" x 14" strips for the top and bottom. Add to the quilt center.

3. For the second border, cut two 1¹/₂" x 13" strips for the side borders and two 1¹/₂" x 16" strips for the top and bottom borders. Add to the quilt center.

4. For the third border, cut two 3¹/₂" x 15" strips for the side borders and two 3¹/₂" x 22" strips for the top and bottom borders. Add to the quilt center.

MAKING THE APPLIQUÉ

Refer to page 30 for appliqué instructions.

1. Cut out and appliqué the sheep, flower, and bird.

2. To make the sheep's ear, cut two ear shapes. Sew the ears, right sides together, around the curved edges. Turn right side out. Sew the ear onto the sheep as shown on page 53. Fold the ear back over the stitched edge and tack down. The ear will be three-dimensional after it's sewn on.

3. Embroider the sheep's nose and eye. See Toolbox, page 32, for instructions to make the embroidery stitches.

FINISHING

1. Layer, baste, and then either hand quilt or machine quilt the top. When marking the border, use the template pattern for the star and place it randomly on the border. Mark the stars, and quilt around them using perle cotton #8.

2. Add binding.

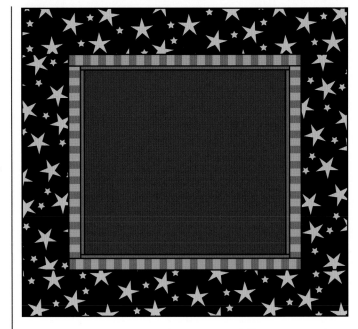

CLOUD QUILTING PATTERN
Enlarge 170%

BIRD
Enlarge 170%

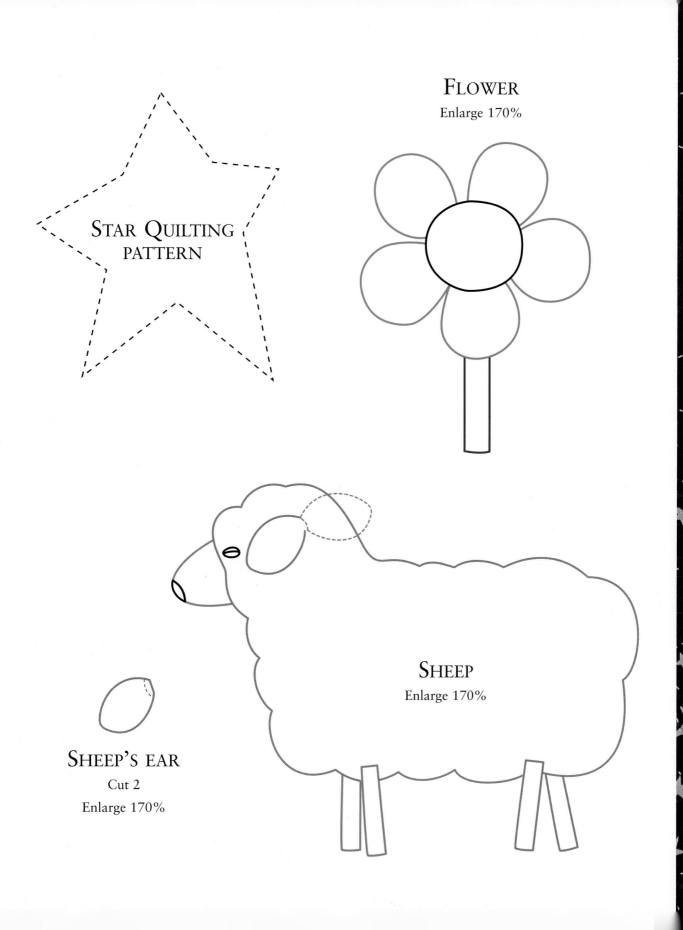

FLOWER
Enlarge 170%

STAR QUILTING
PATTERN

SHEEP
Enlarge 170%

SHEEP'S EAR
Cut 2
Enlarge 170%

Barnyard, 1994, 60³/₄" x 60³/₄".
Photo by Jim Ferreira.

Barnyard

I love watching hens and roosters go about their barnyard business. The rooster usually doesn't do much. He just *is*—though he will strut and crow now and then. Hens, on the other hand, are very unpredictable. They'll amble along, then suddenly make a 180° turn when they spot something edible. Such an abrupt about-face inevitably leaves the poor chicks falling all over themselves as they try to keep up with mother.

One Easter I discovered a collection of seven wooden roosters I'd forgotten about. I decided that someday I would make a chicken quilt. This one grew by itself. It started one day when I began sewing Four-Patches; I'd heard this was good for getting the creative juices flowing. I thought I'd make a nice pieced quilt, but the work soon grew tedious since I had no special plan for the project. I knew I'd never have the patience to sew all those Four-Patches to make a full-size quilt so I began adding some triangles from a red fabric I had lots of.

The work was still going too slowly so I put a brown fabric with twigs right over the hole in the middle of the rows of Four-Patches. I noticed when I held the quilt up that the new fabric looked like dirt in a barnyard. Here at last was a place to put my chickens. Quickly I drew some hens and a rooster. The colorful, polka dot fowl grew to be larger than the space of the barnyard and soon they were spilling into the border.

I knew I wanted a free-form border and I thought about adding flowers, but there aren't many flowers where chickens roam since they seem to pick everything apart. I recalled seeing some tiny pink flowers in a barnyard once, but tiny is not my style. Besides, I have no respect for rules or proportions when it comes to borders and I often play with the scale and color of natural objects. So I made some of my own pink flowers, then randomly placed them on a vine with multicolor leaves in between.

With fabric scraps and inspiration from a rooster in my Easter collection, I had a barnyard quilt. Not bad for a city girl!

TOOLS

- 1 yard for center background
- Assorted scraps for appliqués
- 1/3 yard total assorted scraps for Four-Patches
- 5/8 yard for strips around the Four-Patches
- 1 1/4 yards for setting triangles
- 3/4 yard for bias vine on the appliqué border
- 1 1/4 yards for appliqué border
- 1/4 yard for narrow third border
- 3/4 yard for outer border
- 1/2 yard for binding
- 4 1/4 yards for backing
- 73" x 73" thin batting
- Buttons and embroidery thread
- 1/2" bias tape maker

MAKING THE FOUR-PATCH BORDER

For this quilt I began with the Four-Patch border.

1. Cut eighty 2" squares and sew together as shown to make twenty Four-Patch blocks.

Step 1

Step 2

2. Cut two 1" x 3$\frac{1}{2}$" and two 1" x 5$\frac{1}{2}$" strips for each Four-Patch frame, and add as shown to make twenty 5" blocks (finished).

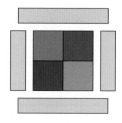

3. To make the Four-Patch border cut four 5$\frac{1}{2}$" setting squares. Cut eight 10" squares; cut diagonally twice for side setting triangles. Cut two 7" squares; cut diagonally once for corner triangles.

4. Sew together as shown, making four side and four corner units.

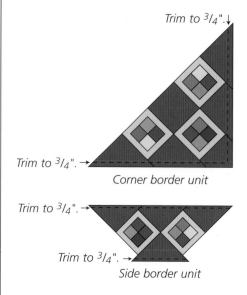

Trim to $^3/_4$".↓

Trim to $^3/_4$". →

Corner border unit

Trim to $^3/_4$". →

Trim to $^3/_4$". →

Side border unit

5. Trim the border units to extend $^3/_4$" beyond the corners of the Four-Patch units so the Four-Patches float. The border will be 8" wide (finished).

6. Cut a 27$^3/_4$" square for the center background. Sew the borders to the center background as shown.

7. Match the center of each side border unit and the center of each side of the background square. Sew together.

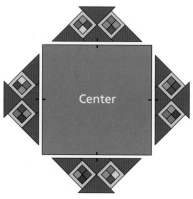

Add side border units.

8. Add each corner border unit, matching the seams of the side units and overlapping the corner of the background square. Sew along the edge of the corner unit. Trim the background corner.

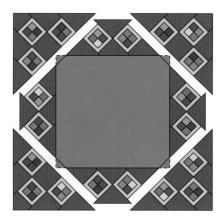

Add corner border units.

9. For the appliqué border, cut seven $5^1/2$"-wide strips. Piece end to end and cut two $5^1/2$" x $43^3/4$" strips for the side borders and two $5^1/2$" x $53^3/4$" strips for the top and bottom borders. Add to the quilt.

10. For the narrow third border, cut six 1"-wide strips. Piece end to end and cut two 1" x $53^3/4$" strips for the side borders and two 1" x $54^3/4$" strips for the top and bottom borders. Add to the quilt.

11. For the outer border, cut six $3^1/2$"-wide strips. Piece end to end and cut two $3^1/2$" x $54^3/4$" strips for the side borders and two $3^1/2$" x $60^3/4$" strips for the top and bottom borders. Add to the quilt.

MAKING THE APPLIQUÉ

Refer to page 30 for appliqué instructions.

1. Cut out and appliqué the hens, rooster, and chicks. Embellish with buttons and embroidery. See Toolbox, page 32, for instructions to make the embroidery stitches.

2. Cut out and appliqué the border flowers and leaves. I put three flowers on each side and four leaves in the dips of the vine. The vine is made from a 1"-wide cut bias strip using a $1/2$" bias tape maker.

FINISHING

Layer, baste, and then either hand quilt or machine quilt the top. Add binding.

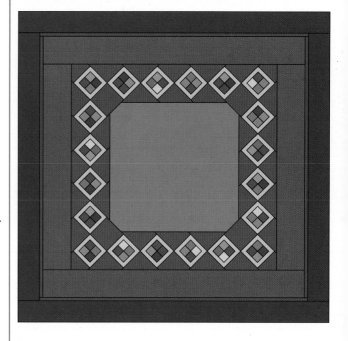

ROOSTER
Enlarge 250%

WORM
Enlarge 250%

HEN

Enlarge 250%

HEN

Enlarge 250%

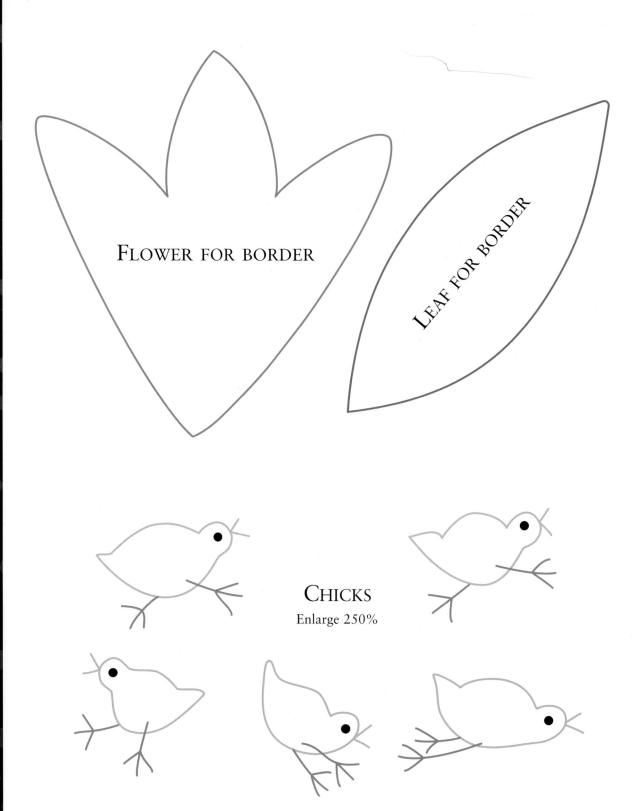

FLOWER FOR BORDER

LEAF FOR BORDER

CHICKS
Enlarge 250%

Index

Other Fine Books From C&T Publishing:

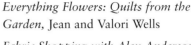

250 Continuous-Line Quilting Designs for Hand, Machine & Long-Arm Quilters, Laura Lee Fritz

Along the Garden Path: More Quilters and Their Gardens, Jean and Valori Wells

An Amish Adventure: 2nd Ed., Roberta Horton

Anatomy of a Doll: The Fabric Sculptor's Handbook, Susanna Oroyan

Appliqué 12 Easy Ways! Charming Quilts, Giftable Projects & Timeless Techniques, Elly Sienkiewicz

The Art of Classic Quiltmaking, Harriet Hargrave and Sharyn Craig

The Art of Machine Piecing: Quality Workmanship Through a Colorful Journey, Sally Collins

Color From the Heart: Seven Great Ways to Make Quilts with Colors You Love, Gai Perry

Color Play: Easy Steps to Imaginative Color in Quilts, Joen Wolfrom

Cotton Candy Quilts: Using Feedsacks, Vintage, and Reproduction Fabrics, Mary Mashuta

Crazy Quilt Handbook, Revised 2nd Ed., Judith Baker Montano

Crazy with Cotton, Diana Leone

Create Your Family Quilt Using State Blocks and Symbols, Barbara Brackman

Curves in Motion: Quilt Designs & Techniques, Judy B. Dales

Cut-Loose Quilts: Stack, Slice, Switch & Sew, Jan Mullen

Designing the Doll: From Concept to Construction, Susanna Oroyan

Do-It-Yourself Framed Quilts: Fast, Fun & Easy Projects, Gai Perry

Easy Pieces: Creative Color Play with Two Simple Blocks, Margaret Miller

Endless Possibilities: Using NO-FAIL Methods, Nancy Johnson-Srebro

Everything Flowers: Quilts from the Garden, Jean and Valori Wells

Fabric Shopping with Alex Anderson, Seven Projects to Help You: Make Successful Choices, Build Your Confidence, Add to Your Fabric Stash, Alex Anderson

Fancy Appliqué: 12 Lessons to Enhance Your Skills, Elly Sienkiewicz

Fantastic Fabric Folding: Innovative Quilting Projects, Rebecca Wat

Fantastic Figures: Ideas & Techniques Using the New Clays, Susanna Oroyan

Finishing the Figure: Doll Costuming • Embellishments • Accessories, Susanna Oroyan

Freddy's House: Brilliant Color in Quilts, Freddy Moran

From Fiber to Fabric: The Essential Guide to Quiltmaking Textiles, Harriet Hargrave

Ghost Layers & Color Washes: Three Steps to Spectacular Quilts, Katie Pasquini Masopust

Great Lakes, Great Quilts: 12 Projects Celebrating Quilting Traditions, Marsha MacDowell, ed.

Hand Appliqué with Alex Anderson: Seven Projects for Hand Appliqué, Alex Anderson

Hand Quilting with Alex Anderson: Six Projects for Hand Quilters, Alex Anderson

Heirloom Machine Quilting, Third Ed., Harriet Hargrave

Imagery on Fabric: A Complete Surface Design Handbook, Second Ed., Jean Ray Laury

In the Nursery: Creative Quilts and Designer Touches, Jennifer Sampou & Carolyn Schmitz

Jacobean Rhapsodies: Composing with 28 Appliqué Designs, Patricia B. Campbell & Mimi Ayars

Laurel Burch Quilts: Kindred Creatures, Laurel Burch

Lone Star Quilts and Beyond: Projects and Inspiration, Jan Krentz

For more information write for a free catalog:

C&T Publishing, Inc.
P.O. Box 1456
Lafayette, CA 94549
(800) 284-1114
e-mail: ctinfo@ctpub.com
website: www.ctpub.com

For quilting supplies:
Cotton Patch Mail Order
3405 Hall Lane, Dept. CTB
Lafayette, CA 94549
(800) 835-4418
(925) 283-7883
e-mail: quiltusa@yahoo.com
website: www.quiltusa.com

Photo by Ingrid Becker

"The longer I live the more I realize what a blessing it's been not to have attended art school or received formal training in textiles. Sure, I'd probably be more skilled and perhaps I wouldn't have spent so long figuring out techniques. On the other hand, I've had a wonderful time throughout my life trying out new skills in needlework, and the process has always seemed new and exciting. Now I'm only bored when I don't have some needlework in my hands."

Self-taught folk artist, dollmaker and quilter Kristina Becker believes the best art comes from within. Kristina has been sewing since she was five and has always enjoyed making patterns, as she says, "from my own thoughts." The motifs for her colorful and whimsical appliqués are inspired by the birds and cats in her neighborhood. If you take time to really "listen" to what's going on in these quilts you'll see that each one tells a story.

For eight years Kristina co-owned a quilting store in Pleasanton, California, where she and her partner, Nancy Taylor, fostered a thriving community of quilters. After they sold the shop in 1988 Kristina began focusing exclusively on the original appliqué quilts featured in this book.

Kristina hopes that by sharing some of her own ways of working she will inspire other quilters and artists to have more fun with their art, to break free from patterns, and create something all their own.